Pluviculture

THE ART OF
MAKING IT RAIN

The Amazing, Mysterious,
True Life of
Charles Mallory Hatfield

WIZARD

LARRY DANE BRIMNER

CALKINS CREEK
AN IMPRINT OF HIGHLIGHTS
Honesdale, Pennsylvania

FOR

CAROLYN P. YODER

DROUGHT

Charles Mallory Hatfield's camp, on a ridge above the northern shore of Morena Reservoir in the backcountry of San Diego County, California, resembled a military outpost. In a way, that is exactly what it was on New Year's Day 1916. Surrounded by a perimeter fence, two white munitions tents glinted in the morning sun. One served as an office and sleeping quarters for the two men manning the camp: Hatfield, age forty, and his twenty-five-year-old brother Joel. The other was used to store their supplies and at least twenty-three secret chemicals. An observation tower, wrapped in heavy, black tar paper for privacy, had been erected a few yards away. The platform stood a dozen or so feet above the ground. Charles Hatfield, wearing a fedora and carrying a rifle, could be seen from time to time patrolling the fence, intent on keeping unwanted visitors at a distance.

A camp similar to the one Hatfield
set up above the shore of Morena
Reservoir. This one dates from
1924. Note the tar-paper wrap
around the tower. Hatfield was
intent on keeping his process and
chemical formula secret.

His was not a usual war. His was a fight against drought that plagued the West and brought crop failure to farmers throughout much of the United States. Charles Hatfield was a rainmaker, although he bristled at the term. He never claimed to *make* rain. He was, instead, a rain inducer or coaxer. He used his secret concoction of chemicals to attract clouds and compel them to give up their moisture.

In early December 1915, Hatfield received a telegram from San Diego's city council. They wanted to talk. At the time, the city was hosting the Panama-California Exposition to celebrate the opening of the Panama Canal. The event was also meant to show off San Diego as the first U.S. port of call that ships heading north would reach after passing westbound through the canal. Political leaders and real estate moguls alike hoped the exposition would present the city at its finest to draw new residents and investors to the area. San Diego had dreams of overtaking Los Angeles as California's most populated city. To accommodate more people, San Diego's leaders realized they would need a reliable and abundant source of water. Its average rainfall of around ten inches each year means it is a semiarid desert. The area historically had experienced long periods of drought. Although it had a system of aqueducts and man-made lakes in place, few if any of these reservoirs had ever been filled to capacity. Certainly, the city's Morena Reservoir, begun in 1897 and completed in 1912, had never received enough rainfall to fill it. With five billion gallons of water retained behind its dam, the reservoir was sitting at only one-third full.

Despite the city's close-to-normal rainfall pattern and nearly average precipitation totals for the year, San Diego's leaders began talking of drought that fall. A *San Diego Union* article from early November claimed "the first rainfall of the season fell last night . . . [and] broke the longest dry spell in the history of San Diego weather during the past 43 years." Considering the city's rainfall totals, the article wasn't exactly accurate. However, the *San Diego Union* and its sister newspaper, the *Evening Tribune*, were owned by John D. Spreckels. At one time or another, he counted among his local holdings large swaths of real estate, the city's electric street-railway system, the Southern California Mountain Water Company (which built Morena Reservoir and was the city's largest, privately owned utility until he sold it to the city for $4 million in 1914), and several downtown buildings. A millionaire many times over and son of Claus Spreckels, who had made a fortune in sugar, John Spreckels didn't hesitate to use his newspapers to promote his views and for his own financial gain. Spreckels was one of two of the most prominent and powerful businessmen in San Diego. The other was Elisha Babcock, who owned four thousand acres of oceanfront property and built, along with Spreckels, the city's grandest hotel, the Hotel del Coronado. Spreckels's views and his newspapers' opinions were always considered by local politicians. Both Spreckels and Babcock knew there was money to be made if only San Diego had water, and lots of it, and talk of drought was one way to spur the city's political leaders to look for sources other than those already in use.

Almost immediately, Shelley Higgins, the assistant city attorney, echoed the *Union*, saying the water supply in the reservoirs had dwindled to an alarming degree. One reservoir was described as being as shallow as a pane of glass. Rural ranchers regularly drew off much,

The Panama-California Exposition was meant to show off the port city of San Diego at its finest. Because the exposition featured exhibits from other countries, it was renamed the Panama-California International Exposition in 1916.

if not most, of the water flowing in the San Diego River, leaving it a mere trickle by the time it reached the ocean. Terence B. Cosgrove, the city attorney, filed a lawsuit against the ranchers. He claimed that on the basis of an old grant from the king of Spain, the full flow of the river belonged to the city and not to rural landowners. Legal battles over water in the American Southwest were common, and plaintiffs often suggested their wells were dry even when they weren't.

The recent surge in growth had placed new demands on San Diego's water supply, and this worried businessmen like Spreckels and Babcock; therefore, it worried politicians. The town's future depended on water. With plans to extend the exposition another year and memories of a seven-year drought in the 1890s, the city council seemed close to desperation.

A down-on-his-luck Englishman, Frederick "Fred" A. Binney, believed in science and in mankind's ability to mold and control nature. He had lost his own citrus orchard a short distance east of San Diego to a winter dry spell. Having followed Charles Hatfield's rainmaking career over the years, he was convinced that Hatfield held the scientific key to ending drought. With a keen sense of how he might make some money, he appointed himself Hatfield's promoter and began taking out advertisements for Hatfield's services in newspapers throughout California. Hatfield, who always prided himself on his integrity and honesty, accepted the help despite Binney's shady reputation. Binney was known in real estate circles for being less than honest, sometimes placing his crude, handmade "For Sale" signs on property that wasn't his to sell. Expecting to receive a percentage of any deals Hatfield

A system of aqueducts and a flume transported water from the mountains to San Diego. The 35.6-mile flume, shown here, was an open wooden ditch that crossed ravines and canyons by means of trestles to keep the slope constant. To celebrate its opening on February 22, 1889, California governor R. W. Waterman and other dignitaries floated down the recently completed flume in flat-bottomed boats. City dwellers often hosted flume-floating parties where they would dress up in their Sunday finest and let the flow of the water carry them downhill in small boats.

The Hotel del Coronado in 1895. The beachside hotel still stands today and boasts a supposedly haunted room under the eaves.

(Right) Charles Hatfield in 1905, age thirty

(Bottom) Paul, Hatfield's younger brother and usually his assistant, at age twenty-one

struck, Binney contacted the city council in 1912 on behalf of the rain-coaxer. He was turned away. His reputation had preceded him, and he met with a skeptical audience.

Still, Binney persisted, as did Hatfield and his younger brother Paul who usually acted as Hatfield's assistant in the rain-coaxing business. In February 1912, Paul proposed to the chamber of commerce of Escondido, a small farming village in inland San Diego County, that he and his older brother would bring four and one-half inches of rain to the county between February 8 and May 1. When his offer wasn't accepted right away, he renewed it by writing in early March, promising three inches of rainfall by the end of April at $1,000 an inch. "My brother and myself," he wrote, "have contracted fourteen commercial [agreements] and filled each and every one with satisfactory results. We like nothing better than the time of drought or dry spells to begin our work." January and February 1912 had been "dreadfully dry," according to a *San Bernardino Sun* article quoted in San Diego's *Evening Tribune.*

Although Escondido's chamber didn't appear eager to sign with the Hatfield brothers, other areas of Southern California responded to Binney's advertisements. Ranchers and landowners in Hemet, California, east of Los Angeles, sent for Charles Hatfield on March 1 and agreed to pay him $4,000 if 4 inches of rain fell in the next two months. Even before the brothers could set up their moisture-attracting apparatus, rain began to fall. By the end of April, 7.2 inches of rain were measured, breaking area records, and the reservoir in Hemet was almost filled. The folks in Hemet were so pleased that they contracted with

the brothers for the coming winter on the same terms. This prompted the *San Bernardino Sun* to speculate, "Either he is a scientist without honor in his own country, or Hatfield, the rainmaker, plays in most amazing luck."

Each successful rain-producing demonstration brought a new flood of inquiries, some from as far away as South Africa. Following his success in Hemet, Hatfield put up three evaporation towers in Carlsbad, Texas, where the San Angelo Chamber of Commerce had hired him to break a long dry spell and save the withering grain and cotton crops. From June and into July, he and Paul worked day and night tending the pans that held the secret concoction of chemicals. The skies opened and by the time the rain stopped falling, more than three inches were measured.

Hatfield returned to California. In April 1913, he traveled to San Diego to talk with a group of business leaders who were interested in hiring him. In explaining his process to the Wide Awake Improvement Association, he said, "It is simply a matter of working in harmony with the natural elements. . . . There are times when the clouds need tickling. If one knows how to tease or coax them a trifle, the results are often pleasing." He knew there were skeptics and others who believed he must be a fanatic with some strange, supernatural power, but he explained that both notions were wrong. He was not a fanatic, and he possessed no supernatural power. His knowledge and ability resulted from studying "nature and [working] with her in attracting elements over a certain locality which will develop into

"THERE ARE TIMES WHEN THE CLOUDS NEED TICKLING."

20

rainfall." By this time, Hatfield had conducted successful experiments in Los Angeles and other parts of California, Texas, Oregon, and beyond.

Binney again offered Hatfield's services to San Diego in June 1914, writing that, for $500, Hatfield would cause five inches of rain to fall in the Morena Reservoir watershed between then and November. These were the city's dry months. He also asked the city to guarantee Hatfield an additional sum of $1,000 per inch for up to ten inches beyond the five-inch mark. The issue was referred to the city's water department, which was charged with reporting to the council. The Wide Awake Improvement Association took up the cause, writing to council members "that no harm could come from giving Hatfield a chance to fulfill such a contract, and that if he were successful, it would be worth a great deal more than $10,000 to the city."

The water department's assistant superintendent, H. A. Whitney, didn't share the association's enthusiasm. He commented, "If Hatfield can refer to some first class hydraulic engineer to prove that he can produce rain, . . . I will be in favor of making a contract with him." Getting an endorsement from an engineer or a high-ranking official from the United States Weather Bureau would be nearly impossible. Engineers, weathermen, and other men of science believed Hatfield was a flimflam man, a practitioner of hocus-pocus. Binney argued that the water department's request didn't make sense. A hydraulic engineer is responsible for taking water from the ground and conserving it. "What does he know . . . about getting it from the air?" Binney asked. The city council turned down Hatfield's offer, preferring to leave it to nature to provide adequate rainfall.

By December 1915, San Diego's city council had changed its position. Council members had heard business leaders, including Spreckels and Babcock, who supported extending the Panama-California Exposition another year and wished to show off the city to visitors as a green oasis with abundant water. The council had read articles in the *Union* and *Evening Tribune* that talked of drought, and sent word to Hatfield that it wished to meet with him. Described inaccurately in the *San Diego Union* as "the inventor of a rainmaking machine"—there was no machine—Hatfield offered to produce forty inches of rain for the city for free but asked it to guarantee payment of "$1000 for each inch of rain produced over forty and under fifty [inches]." Ten thousand dollars! To offer proof that he was legitimate and his word was good, he sent a photograph of a lake he claimed to have filled to overflowing in California's Central Valley.

When Hatfield met with the mayor and council on December 9, he surprised them. He was self-assured and well-spoken, without any of the bluster of a confidence man, a swindler. They advised him to put together a proposal in writing, which he did. He offered them three options. The first was the same as his original proposition: to deliver forty inches of rain within a year free of charge. For any amount above that quantity to fifty inches, he would bill the city $1,000 per inch. The second was to produce thirty inches of rain within six months for free, but he would be paid $500 for each inch over that amount to fifty inches. The third of his proposals was to fill Morena Reservoir for $10,000. The meeting was attended by Mayor Edward Capps, and five councilmen: Herbert R. Fay, Walter Moore, Percy Benbough, Henry

The Panama-California International Exposition capitalized on San Diego's Spanish heritage with newly built structures in the Spanish Colonial Revival style. The California Building, opposite, was influenced by the designs of Mexican churches and served as the entrance to the exposition. Today it houses the San Diego Museum of Man.

Charles Hatfield (on ladder) at work constructing a tower. In this staged photograph, his assistant was likely Paul, though he was not identified.

Manney, and Otto Schmidt. City manager Fred Lockwood, city attorney Terence Cosgrove, and assistant city attorney Shelley Higgins were also in the council chambers. Councilman Moore was in favor of accepting Hatfield's offer to fill Morena Reservoir, saying, "He will have to put ten billion gallons of water in it, which would cost the city one-tenth of a cent per thousand gallons; if he fails to fulfill his contract, the city isn't out anything. It's head[s], the city wins; tails, Hatfield loses." When asked if a contract with Hatfield would be legal, the city attorney grinned, then chose his words carefully and spoke slowly: "If Hatfield fills Morena, I guess there would be no doubt about the legality."

DAY AND NIGHT, THE BROTHERS CONTINUED THEIR VAPOROUS ASSAULT ON THE SKIES.

It was a question of *if*.

On December 13, 1915, in a vote of 4 to 1, San Diego's council members ordered the city attorney to prepare a contract with Hatfield to fill Morena Reservoir to overflowing. They would give the rain-coaxer until December 20, 1916, to do it—just over a year. If he succeeded, the city agreed it would pay him $10,000. If he failed, San Diego would owe Hatfield nothing. Only Councilman Fay voted against it. He said he thought the entire business was foolishness. Hatfield, who was present during the council vote, asked that he be given credit for any water drawn out of the reservoir for consumption during the year. The council agreed.

Hatfield left council chambers that morning saying he would get his moisture-accelerating equipment together and begin work by the start of the year. Indeed, he was in such a hurry to get busy that he didn't bother to wait for a written agreement. So confident was he that he told the press on December 21 he would earn the $10,000 offered by the city. Then he and his youngest brother, Joel, began the long, slow trek over rugged, mountainous terrain to Morena Reservoir, some sixty miles east of town. Paul usually would have assisted his brother. With no rainmaking contracts since the spring of 1914, however, Hatfield and Paul had returned to their first jobs: selling sewing machines in Los Angeles. To earn money in order to keep the Morena camp supplied until Hatfield could bring home the big paycheck, Paul remained in Los Angeles.

By New Year's Day, Hatfield and Joel had established their camp, erected a tower, and were at work at Morena Reservoir.

In no time, the acrid fumes of evaporating chemicals were rising into the atmosphere that first Saturday of 1916. Day and night, the brothers continued their vaporous assault on the skies. A mile or so away in the dam keeper's cottage, Seth Swenson and his wife, Maggie, reported that the stench was overpowering. They were Hatfield's link via telephone to the city, and Seth would monitor the reservoir's gauges. Another observer said the air smelled so bad, the clouds would have to rain in self-defense.

Rain?

A light drizzle began to fall early the morning of January 4.

2

LIGHTNING

From the very beginning, it seemed as if Charles Hatfield would have a kinship to drought and rain. He was born into a Quaker family in Fort Scott, Kansas, on July 15, 1875, the third child of Stephen and Marie Hatfield. A family myth suggests his birth was announced by a cloudburst of monumental proportions and a lightning strike that killed four cattle. Rain fell in such quantities that dusty streets turned into muddy rivers, stranding a westward-bound wagon train and halting railroad service for several days. Exactly when people began to spin this yarn, no one is sure, but Kansas was in a drought in 1874 and 1875, accompanied by an invasion of locusts that damaged crops. "It was a bad time and drove a lot of settlers" to abandon their farms and return to the East. As for young Hatfield's birth ending the drought with a cloudburst, the *Fort Scott Daily Monitor* reported no rain for July 15,

Family lore claimed that Hatfield broke a dry spell, complete with lightning, when he entered the world. Was he responsible for the storms that brought rain before his birth?

and a temperature reading of "99° in the shade . . . the warmest day of the season." In the days just before his birth, however, a lightning storm did strike the city and flooding was extensive. "The regular train . . . for the east was delayed . . . , the rain having washed away a bridge near Osage Mission." The day before he was born, the *Monitor* declared, "Rain! rain!! rain!!! No drouth [*sic*] in Kansas this year." Did Hatfield's arrival end the dry spell, or was it coincidence that these events occurred in the days just before his birth?

Whether or not his birth influenced the weather, young Hatfield was born into a nomadic family. His father, Stephen, married Marie Mallory in 1869 in Davenport, Iowa. He was a salesman with the Singer Sewing Company and made a good living, but he also seemed rootless. Originally from New York, he had lived in Michigan before meeting Marie. In 1870, they welcomed the birth of a son, Stephen Girard. A daughter, Phoebe, followed in 1872. A short while after Phoebe's birth, Stephen moved the family to Fort Scott, Kansas. Here he established his own sewing machine agency. In 1875, however, he sold the agency and used the money from its sale to build a large house for his growing family. From this point on, the elder Stephen's livelihood would be earned as a land speculator—buying property, building houses, and selling them at a profit. He seemed to be always on the lookout for the next sure investment.

By the time young Charles was five in 1880, the Fort Scott

Marie Mallory Hatfield in an undated photo

30

house had been sold and the family moved to Minneapolis, Minnesota, where the number of children increased by four, all boys. Only two survived infancy: Paul (born in 1886) and Joel (born in 1890). Shortly after Joel's birth, Stephen decided it was time for another move, this time to the latest boomtown: San Diego, California.

In San Diego, Stephen bought three lots and quickly built houses upon them. He also purchased a forty-acre olive ranch in a rural area north of San Diego. Unfortunately, by the time the family arrived, San Diego's boom was already in decline, with people favoring Los Angeles. Roughly 120 miles to the north, this city offered better rail connections than San Diego. Before the year's end, Stephen had followed the northward migration. He moved his family to an imposing house on a ten-acre apricot ranch, where they were one of the first families to live in what was then called Cahuenga Valley. Finding that farming was too much at the mercy of the weather, he quickly sold the orchard and relocated first to South Pasadena and then to Pasadena, both a short distance east of Los Angeles. His only tie now to San Diego was the olive ranch, which he had kept.

In Los Angeles, Charles Hatfield left school at the end of ninth grade. Following his father's advice, he went to work for the Robert B. Moorhead Agency selling New Home Sewing Machines. His father had insisted that all his sons learn how to take apart, repair, and reassemble these machines as a path to a career and prosperity.

The Quaker beliefs in self-reliance, self-determination, and individualism proved a good foundation for Hatfield. In a starched shirt

Stephen Hatfield moved his family from San Diego to an impressive house and apricot ranch in Cahuenga Valley (now Hollywood). This photo shows the young orchard in 1891.

and pressed suit, the young man was a striking figure standing on a porch, and he proved to be an even better salesman than his father. He had a charm that made people like him. For an average sale, he pocketed $10 to $15, and he was soon bringing in $125 a month. When asked once what he did when he saw a "No Peddlers" sign beside a door, he said he ignored it. Continuing to live at home, he spent his money on nice suits, silk ties, and fancy hats.

Away from work, though, he was quiet and bookish by nature. He never forgot the talk of drought in Los Angeles and before that, as a boy in San Diego, Minnesota, and Kansas. He remembered the terrible years of drought throughout Southern California in the early and mid-1890s. The Hatfields' apricot and olive crops had suffered during these dry spells. He also had read about farmers who had lost everything because the weather had not cooperated and provided sufficient rainfall. He spent long hours at the Los Angeles Public Library, where he read about his singular obsession: people's attempt to control nature.

Hatfield, now twenty-six, began his rain-coaxing experiments when he visited his father's San Diego County olive ranch in 1902. In April, atop a windmill tower some thirty feet above the ground, he set up several metal pans into which he poured a mixture of chemicals and water. He placed an electric heater beneath the pans and watched as a thin wisp of vapor rose into the morning air. To anybody passing by, the rising gas was barely noticeable—except for its overpowering stench. He spent most of the morning stirring the chemicals, replacing them when necessary, and waiting. Before long, a misty fog began to fill the valley, and by noon a light drizzle started to fall. After the rain cleared, Hatfield checked his rain gauge and noted that three-hundredths of an inch had fallen. He had surprised himself, but also figured he was on to something.

His father thought Hatfield's interest in artificial methods of rain production was a waste of time. Stephen encouraged him to focus on the sewing machine business. His mother, though, seemed to sense that he was destined for greater things and took a quiet pride in his endeavors. His boss, Robert Moorhead, also was interested in the young man's obsession. He didn't force strict hours on Hatfield as long as he brought in the sales. This Hatfield did, allowing him frequent opportunities to test his theories quietly in San Diego County.

Hatfield continued his experiments at the ranch throughout 1902 and 1903, when he wasn't selling sewing machines in Los Angeles. In early January 1904, the *Pacific Rural Press* announced, "The drought is seriously retarding plowing and seeding. Feed is becoming very scarce, and, although there is a fair supply of last season's hay in most places, the long continued use of dry feed has seriously affected cattle. The water supply is failing rapidly, owing to heavy irrigation of orchards." By the end of the month, Los Angeles clergymen had declared Sunday, January 31, a day to pray for rain. Two days later, Hatfield and his brother Paul loaded a horse-drawn wagon with lumber, metal pans, and other supplies. They headed into the hills northeast of Los Angeles, where they built a tower similar to the windmill frame he had used in

CHARLES MALLORY HAT-
FIELD

*Sketched by an "Examiner" Staff
Artist*

Before photographs were common in newspapers, artists' sketches were published. Here is an artist's take on Hatfield in 1905 after he claimed his $50 prize.

San Diego. By nightfall, the secret formula was warming in evaporation trays.

Money was riding on this test of Hatfield's theory. His boss, Robert Moorhead, had convinced several Los Angeles merchants to go in with him and put up a prize of $50 if Hatfield could make it rain. The *Los Angeles Herald* reported, "Rainmaker Hatfield is a sewing machine solicitor by day. By night he delves into the mysteries of . . . air strata and all the queer habits of the realm above. For years he studied the subject before he ventured on a hypothesis. Then he made up his mind that what was needed to 'prime' the pumps of heaven was an attack by persuasive fumes. So Rainmaker Hatfield got him a tank, mixed up a dose for J. Pluvius and hoisted it skyward by a method known only to himself." (In Roman mythology, J. Pluvius or Jupiter Pluvius was the king of gods and giver of rain.)

Returning to Los Angeles on February 7, Hatfield told reporters, "When I started out . . . conditions were extremely unfavorable for me. . . . At 7:30 Thursday night the rain began, and at 10:30 o'clock there set in a heavy downpour, which continued until 2 o'clock Friday morning. . . . Friday morning at 11:30 the rain began again and continued in showers until 8:30 o'clock at night." He was modest and willing to share credit for the downpour with the preachers who had prayed for rain on January 31. Nor did he take credit for rainfall along the coast of Oregon. "I don't claim full credit for the downpour," he said, "but I do say that I was responsible for holding the storm in Southern California as long as it stayed." The sewing machine salesman believed he was responsible for heavier rainfall in Los Angeles than would have occurred had he not been releasing his chemical mixture into the heavens, and he wanted recognition for that. "My process," he explained, "is to work upon the humidity of the atmosphere. I have tried it eighteen times and have recorded only one failure." After collecting his $50 prize, he returned to selling sewing machines—and waiting for the next call to break a dry spell.

George E. Franklin of the U.S. Weather Bureau in Los Angeles had predicted that precipitation would miss the city. He moved quickly to squelch any notion that the rainfall was the result of Hatfield's chemical activities. Franklin, whom the *Los Angeles Herald* called the "Weather Guesser," said, "I would not say that the preachers or the rainmaker is responsible for the rain. Personally I am inclined to think we should thank that power which for decades past has controlled such things. It seems queer to me that a man by a chemical assault on the heavens in the foothills in Southern California should be responsible for a storm which began 'way up on the Oregon coast."

Nonetheless, the Spring Street businessmen in Los Angeles who had challenged Hatfield on a no-rain, no-pay basis were satisfied. "Long live Rainmaker Hatfield, and may he reign longer!" they cheered, making a play on words. James M. Barnett of Barnett & Gude (one of the firms that contributed to the $50 prize) said, "We're satisfied. We've had the rain within the scheduled time and Hatfield gets the cash.

The preachers and providence don't enter into this matter with us. Hatfield did it with his little tank. Bully for Hatfield!"

For all the attention he got, George Franklin may as well have been speaking to himself.

Hatfield's mother, Marie, proudly posed for the *Los Angeles Times* in the days following his return. She told the reporter that her son had struggled against the prejudices of people like Franklin but was determined to prove the skeptics wrong. She claimed he must be aided by some divine power.

Franklin was further frustrated when, in December, Hatfield made a public proposition to bring eighteen inches of rain between mid-December and May 1, 1905, for $1,000. Franklin had issued a prediction of fair weather and sunshine when the sky began to weep. He called Hatfield to complain, saying, "This thing has got to stop at once.... My reputation is already ruined. The way that the streets were flooded and the merchants sold umbrellas is enough to convince any one [*sic*] that my word is not good for anything." Hatfield replied, "Well, you do not need to get mad about it.... If you ever make a rain prediction let me know and I shall be glad to help you out."

On December 15, 1904, he set up his cloud-attracting apparatus on the grounds of Esperanza Sanitarium, a hospital for people with lung diseases. (*Esperanza* is a Spanish word that means "hope.") The hospital was located in the foothills northeast of Los Angeles, near Altadena. Rain began to fall almost immediately and continued through Christmas. The *Los Angeles Examiner* praised the results by printing a poem in honor of the rain-coaxer:

His name is Hatfield—
Just simply Hatfield!
The only name that Californians speak;
Oh, Mister Hatfield,
Here's to you, Hatfield—
God bless you for that thankful heavenly leak!

Soon, though, local newspapers were pleading with him to give them a dry, sunny day on Monday, January 2, 1905, so the annual Tournament of Roses Parade could go on as scheduled in Pasadena. When rain fell in the morning but cleared in time for the parade, organizers publicly expressed thanks.

The rain continued to fall in record quantities through January, February, and March 1905. By March 30, officials had measured 18.22 inches for Los Angeles. The *Los Angeles Herald* declared that twenty-nine-year-old Hatfield had won his $1,000 prize, only now the newspaper referred to him as the "Wizard of Esperanza"—the Wizard of Hope.

After his $1,000 wager, Hatfield's fame spread and his fortunes grew. In Los Angeles, the word *raining* was routinely replaced with *Hatfielding*. Umbrellas were sold not as mere *umbrellas* but as "Genuine 'Hatfield' Umbrellas," and they were expensive.

Despite the attention, Hatfield wanted more than anything to be taken seriously. He decided to build on the publicity by offering a series of lectures around the state that came complete with a demonstration using chemicals and test tubes. He now billed himself as Professor

In an undated photograph, Charles Hatfield poses in front of two tents and his trademark towers.

Charles Hatfield, and his talks were popular, each one bringing more job offers. Despite the fact that his demonstrations never revealed his secret for attracting moisture from clouds and he often used language his audiences didn't understand, he offered hope. In a landscape where farmers were dependent on rainfall and usually deeply in debt, hope was priceless—although Hatfield usually priced it by the inch. His success, however, raised the ire of officials at every level of the U.S. Weather Bureau, and they took every opportunity to denounce him as a fraud.

In June 1906, Hatfield and Paul were on the deck of the steamer *Selkirk* as it docked in Dawson City, Canada. The brothers had been hired to break a drought in the Yukon Territory. Not everyone was happy about the contract. George E. Foster, a member of the Canadian House of Commons, worried that Hatfield's tampering with nature might pull the plug on the skies and result in worldwide catastrophic dangers. In the end, Foster need not have worried. Hatfield wasn't able to produce rain in the quantities his employers wished. He left Dawson City with only enough to cover his expenses: $1,100. Even so, he argued that he hadn't failed; he said he had produced rain on thirty-six of his forty-four workdays, just not enough to satisfy the mine operators who had hired him.

After returning to California from Dawson City, Hatfield continued to collect headlines and hefty fees. He also met and married Maybelle Rulon, a divorced mother of two, in San Diego. His brother Paul married Maybelle's younger sister, Edna. The foursome moved north, where Hatfield, his wife, and her two children settled into a bungalow

For publicity, Hatfield mixes chemicals. However, he never used these chemicals in his secret formula.

DAWSON, SHOWING YUKON AND KLONDYKE RIVERS, AND "THE SLIDE."

Arrived Here at 9 P.M. June 5th 1906 Charlie.

In June 1906, Hatfield and Paul
arrived in Dawson City where mine
owners had hired them to produce
rain for their mining operations.

in the Eagle Rock section of Los Angeles. Paul and Edna moved into a house nearby. Between rainmaking engagements, Paul took whatever work he could find, while Hatfield met with and entertained questions from reporters to keep his name before the public.

As the 1900s rolled on, he told reporters of lucrative foreign contracts that were in the works: ridding London of its fog, irrigating the Sahara, and breaking droughts in South Africa. However, when prospective employers checked with the U.S. Weather Bureau for references, Willis L. Moore, chief of the agency since 1895, told them that Hatfield was practicing deception on a grand order. These foreign contracts never became reality.

After returning to California from the Yukon Territory, Hatfield married Maybelle Rulon. They moved, with her two children from an earlier marriage, to this house in the Eagle Rock section of Los Angeles.

THUNDER

People have tried to control the weather from the very earliest times. Native American tribes danced and burned tobacco to make the heavens spill their moisture. Tribesmen in Africa, Asia, and Australia spat water into the air or covered themselves with feathers and blood in rituals that were believed to bring rain. At the first sight of gray skies in eighteenth-century Europe, bell ringers would race to church towers to ring rain from above. This practice eventually was stopped in England because bell ringers routinely were being killed by lightning strikes. In California during the 1880s, rainmaker Michael Cahill put forth the idea that rain clouds were formed by high-flying birds such as eagles and condors. He unsuccessfully urged the federal government and the California legislature to breed and train flocks of feathered fowls that could be released to break dry spells.

In the United States during the age of Henry Ford, Thomas Edison, and the Wright brothers in the late 1800s and early 1900s, people began to think there was no limit to what people could achieve through science and modern-day technology. Many serious-minded people believed that control of the country's weather by scientific means was inevitable.

Meteorologist James Pollard Espy advanced the idea of convection as a way to create artificial rain. He had noted that great fires, under the right conditions, may sometimes be followed by rain. If a large column of moist air could be made to rise (convection), a cloud would form and result in rain. He suggested burning forty acres of forested land every twenty miles from west to east during each week of summer in bands from the southern to the northern borders of the United States to create the necessary updraft of air. He was certain rain would follow, but the idea wasn't practical. Also, since weather patterns in the United States usually travel from west to east, it would do little for lands west of the burn zone. When Espy sought funds from the U.S. Congress to test his theory, he was turned away.

James Pollard Espy was convinced that extensive updrafts of warm air, or the process of convection, would create clouds, which in turn would produce rain.

Early observers had noted that rainfall often followed battles. Was there a scientific connection? In 1890, Charles B. Farwell, a U.S. senator from Illinois who owned large land holdings in Texas, pushed Congress to approve $2,000 for experiments in the artificial production of rain.

Robert St. George Dyrenforth, a patent attorney in Washington, D.C., was hired to research and carry out the tests. Dyrenforth favored the concussion, or percussion, method of rainmaking whereby explosives were detonated in the atmosphere to imitate a battlefield. Rather than firing cannons into the air, however, he liked the idea of detonating balloons filled with a volatile mixture of oxygen, hydrogen, and an explosive at high altitude. The thought was that the explosions would create a vortex, or hole, into which moisture would be drawn and fall to the earth as rain.

MANY SERIOUS-MINDED PEOPLE BELIEVED THAT CONTROL OF THE COUNTRY'S WEATHER BY SCIENTIFIC MEANS WAS INEVITABLE.

After initially testing specially made balloons at his home near Washington, to the irritation of his neighbors, Dyrenforth moved his operations to Texas. Accounts of his experiments were carried in newspapers far and wide. In August 1891 at the Nelson Morris ranch near Midland, he set up his equipment: "40 10-foot balloons made, to contain about 600 cubic feet of gas; 28 12-foot balloons, to contain about 1000 cubic feet of gas, and three large balloons . . . to make . . . observations. He also procured several bolts of red cambric [cotton cloth] and enough sticks and twine to make and fly several hundred large kites."

Twelve hours after the balloons were detonated, rain began to fall. The *Boston Weekly Globe* headlines announced: "Rain Made to Order" and "Gen. Dyrenforth Opens the Heavenly Faucets" and "Jack Rabbits on Arid Plains Use Their Ears for Umbrellas." Reporters praised Dyrenforth and his scientific approach to artificial rainmaking.

"Whenever he ordered the dynamite . . . and the explosive balloons to be turned loose upon a clear sky there was certain to be a smart rainfall within 12 hours." The report went on to boast that "this did not happen once or twice or thrice; it happened nine or 10 times, and in a country, too, were [sic] showers of any kind are exceedingly rare, and where good rains are almost unknown." Hearing these accounts, supporters in Congress began talking about releasing even more money to Dyrenforth—up to a million dollars. But many reporters failed to observe Dyrenforth's experiments firsthand; instead they relied on information supplied by Dyrenforth.

Soon other reports began to reach Washington by eyewitness observers. The *San Francisco Chronicle* headline told the story: "Not Makers of Rain." Rainfall had been predicted in the Texas panhandle before the Dyrenforth experiments. The patent attorney claimed, "This portion of the country received the most thorough watering it has had for the last three years, and the reports from incoming cowboys indicate that the storm extended over many hundreds of miles." However, Dyrenforth failed to tell newspaper reporters or Congress that August rain in this area of Texas was a common occurrence. And he didn't mention what eyewitnesses observed—that many balloons and kites never made it aloft because they were damaged, that some caught fire before

Believing in the concussion method of artificial rain, Robert St. George Dyrenforth detonated explosives in the skies over Texas, but his efforts were unsuccessful.

reaching the desired altitude, that at least one drifted away and was found intact ten miles from the Morris ranch, that balloon preparation was chaotic, and, perhaps most damaging, that the first rain fell days before the experiments began.

Dyrenforth had good reason to make his tests sound more successful than they were. By this time, he was using his own money to conduct them. When his questionable success in Midland was followed by out-and-out failures in other parts of Texas, Congress lost interest in the concussion method of rainmaking.

At the same time that Dyrenforth was bombarding the skies over Texas with explosives, Frank Melbourne was boasting that he could produce rain even in Death Valley, California. He never made it to California. He operated in Ohio, where his brother lived, and in Wyoming, where he played on the desperation of ranchers and farmers during long dry spells. He also carried out his work in Kansas and neighboring states. He toted his rainmaking machine in an ordinary-looking black satchel and told people it cost $15,000 to make. Working in secrecy behind the closed doors of a shed or an outbuilding, he charged people $300 to $400 to make it rain. Although it was only the size of a dinner pail, his device required an exhaust pipe that extended more than twelve feet above the shed roof. When asked by a reporter for Ohio's *Marion Daily Star* how he produced rain, he explained, "It is the infusion of certain chemicals in the air through a machine of my own invention."

Melbourne, sometimes called "the Rain King," was a smell-maker.

A gambler, he often made ten times his rainmaking fee in bets

DATES,

SEPTEMBER

22nd to 26th

Inclusive

THE MOST

Wonderful

Inventor

of the

Century.

Frank Mel'ourne, the Rain Wizard.

Melbourne the "Ohio Rain Wizard"

Will be at GOODLAND

Fair Week.

And has contracted to produce a Heavy Rain the last day of the Fair, Sep't 26th.

Governor Humphrey

Will be present one day.

The management of the Fair Association will spare no pains or expense to make this fair the most entertaining of any ever held in western Kansas.

One and One Third Rate

has been secured over the Rock Island.

Alex Martin, Pres.,   Wm. Walker Jr. Sec'y.

SHERMAN COUNTY FARMER Print, Goodland, Kansas.

Gambler Frank Melbourne used chemicals to make the clouds weep and county fairs to increase his fame.

he and his brother made on the side regarding whether or not it would rain. In the summer of 1894, though, his fortunes turned. He failed to produce rain in Nebraska and Colorado, which damaged his reputation. He was discredited further when it was discovered that the dates he said moisture would fall at his command were identical to long-range forecasts in a popular farming almanac. In August, he committed suicide in a Denver hotel. What became of his machine and formula of chemicals? Many speculated they had been stolen, because they were not among his possessions at the hotel.

About this time, several commercial companies around Goodland, Kansas, entered the rainmaking business. None was more prestigious than the Chicago, Rock Island, and Pacific Railway. Employee Clayton B. Jewell asked his bosses for $250 worth of chemicals to experiment with artificial-rain production. A reliable source of rain would mean farmers would have more abundant crops and be able to ship greater quantities of produce over the company's rails. Jewell's bosses not only provided everything he asked for, but they also outfitted a special car for the rainmaker's equipment and use. He began crisscrossing Kansas and neighboring states, his railcar releasing clouds of throat-burning gases. Knowing the importance of showmanship, Jewell often set off Dyrenforth-type explosions or sent rockets skyward. But he was a smell-maker at heart. He claimed to have produced rain thirty-three times in 1893. During the hot, dry summer of 1899, a group of California businessmen invited him to Los Angeles. He scheduled his demonstrations for July 18 and 19, but despite a sixty-hour, nonstop assault on the skies, they remained blue and dry.

Charles Hatfield would have known about these rainmakers from his readings. He spoke of Dyrenforth in respectful tones and corrected newspaper reporters when they inaccurately listed the quantities Jewell used in his Los Angeles experiments. Western newspapers, claiming to have discovered Jewell's formula, printed that it was nothing more than sulfuric acid, zinc, and water. Could these newspaper reports have led to Hatfield's own experimentation with chemicals at the San Diego ranch in 1902 and '03?

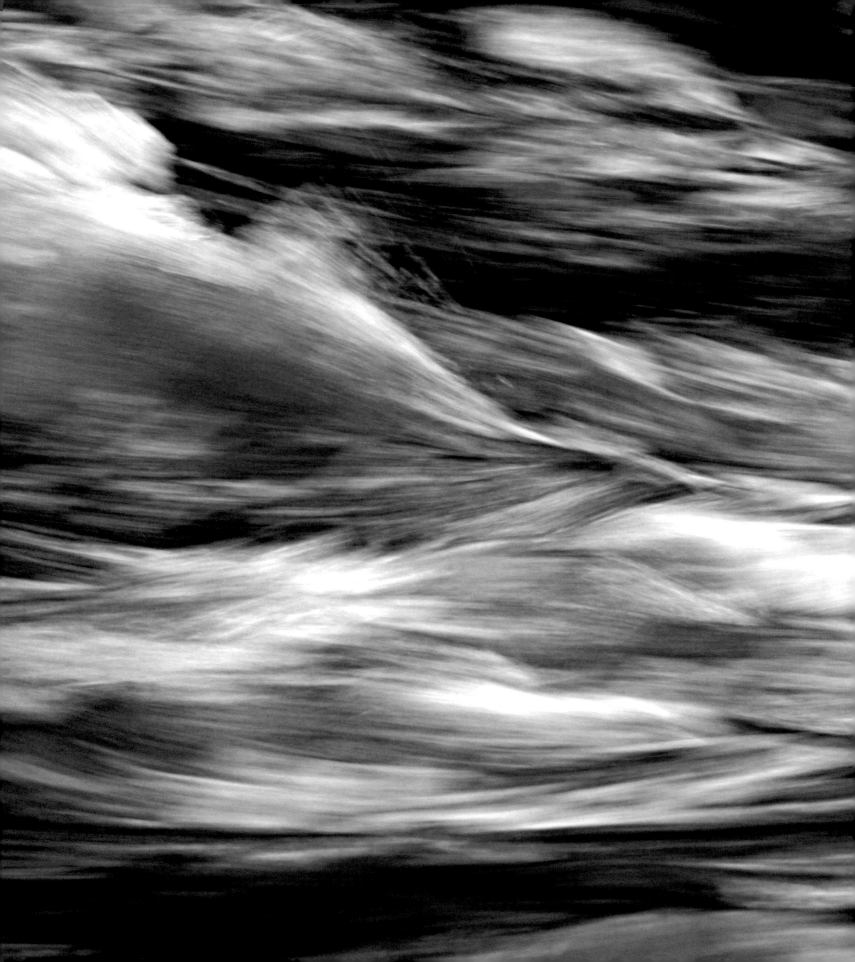

January 4, 1916. Seth Swenson, the dam keeper, telephoned officials in San Diego at 10:30 that morning with news that a light rain began to fall at Morena Reservoir in the early hours and was continuing. Years later, Paul recalled that in order to fill the reservoir, Hatfield had decided "to give them the works." Instead of the usual single chest of chemicals, he'd brought two. There had been rain on New Year's Eve and all the area reservoirs had benefited from it with significant gains in stored water. Hatfield was certain he could reach his goal. That morning, shrouded behind black tar paper, he tended his pans of chemicals on the tower. He was intent on earning the $10,000 paycheck promised by San Diego if he could fill Morena Reservoir to overflowing.

Local newspapers were filled with speculation about what Hatfield was doing in San Diego's backcountry. A few curious folk who had

made the trek to the reservoir reported hearing explosions and seeing rockets launched into the air. One said he'd seen Hatfield looking skyward and waving his arms on the tower while he muttered in a strange language, as if striking a deal with the heavens. When Maggie Swenson, the dam keeper's wife, had asked

Compliments of CHAS. M. HATFIELD

(*Above*) Charles Hatfield's business card

(*Left*) Charles Hatfield checks some of his equipment.

Hatfield how he did his work, he explained simply that he was a scientist and not a magician, and left it at that. Rudolph Wueste, a supervisor with the county's system of reservoirs, suspected that Hatfield used "a compound of hydrogen and zinc." It was all guesswork or outrageous fabrication. Nobody actually got close enough to the camp to see or hear much of anything. Visitors were always met by Hatfield or Joel at the perimeter fence that surrounded their camp. Hatfield was a man of secrets.

Writing about the rain of January 4, the *San Diego Union* reported, "Whether Hatfield's mysterious process is responsible for the downpour, he will get credit for it when next December the increase of water in Morena reservoir during the year is calculated." Amusingly, the *Evening Tribune* accused him of pulling "the wrong switch" because rain totals were greater in Los Angeles than in San Diego. "Official figures give Morena dam a rainfall of .13 of an inch since Saturday [January 1] while Los Angeles in the same time had 2 inches."

The drizzle continued and turned into a daily downpour. By the tenth of the month, it was as if somebody had turned on all the heavenly faucets directly over San Diego.

Rather than relaxing, Hatfield increased his efforts, his cloud-attracting apparatus belching out more smelly fumes than even before. From a distance, one observer noted that Hatfield seemed to work at all hours, day and night, and was receiving quite a drenching himself. At least the heavy rain reduced the number of visitors to the camp.

The skies cleared, briefly, presenting two days of sharp blue and sunshine.

Then on Friday, January 14, a wall of dark gray clouds approached the city from over the Pacific Ocean to the west. By Saturday, Hatfield was on everybody's mind. Was he responsible for the heavy, extended rain? "Here's hoping that it continues to rain so hard that Hatfield will have to build an ark," declared Councilman Benbough. "More power to him—likewise more rain," added Councilman Moore. "Amen," said Councilman Fay. While these city officials would not admit they regarded the rain-coaxer seriously, they agreed that if Morena was filled to overflowing, they would willingly pay him. When asked what he thought about the rain, Herbert Nimmo of the U.S. Weather Bureau in San Diego said, "I'll tell you what I think. . . . I think that we are going to have more rain . . . and that the man who leaves his umbrella at home . . . will be making a mistake." According to the *San Diego Union*, though, "Weatherman Nimmo is inclined to pooh-pooh at Hatfield. He declares that the storm, being widely distributed, is caused by natural conditions."

And the skies continued to weep.

Although he had been told to prepare a contract for Hatfield in December, City Attorney Cosgrove still had not done so. A shrewd politician, he seemed intent on finding a way out of paying Hatfield for anything, not even expenses, which Hatfield was paying himself. On Sunday, January 16, the *San Diego Union* reported that Cosgrove would not draw up a contract between Hatfield and the city until Hatfield provided "him with correct data concerning plans, number of men employed, methods used, and other information." Cosgrove continued, "He will not be required to reveal any secrets, . . . but he must furnish such information as will enable the city to ascertain whether or not the runoff at Morena is the direct results of his rainmaking efforts." He knew it was unprovable.

Even as he spoke with reporters, runoff was flowing from hillsides into all the area's reservoirs, including the Upper Otay and Lower Otay. The Lower Otay Reservoir rose five inches in eight hours. The Sweetwater Reservoir reported that water was rising at half an inch a day. From Morena, Hatfield telephoned to report "seventeen and a half inches of rain in the last five days, and that beats any similar record for this place that I have been able to find." Meanwhile, San Diegans were tired of the endless rain; it had brought the city almost to a standstill. The *Evening Tribune* suggested, "If Hatfield made it rain, he can make a lot of money by stopping it."

By 2:00 a.m., Monday, January 17, the city was consumed by chaos as runoff entered once-empty gullies, canyons, and washes. Now, raging torrents made their way downstream to the city's reservoirs.

When rain began falling in San Diego, many people were caught unaware when normally dry washes became raging torrents of water.

Many of San Diego's backcountry bridges—including this railroad bridge—were swept away.

The San Diego River, usually just a trickle, breached its banks and stretched a mile across from side to side. Hillsides collapsed and roadways gave way. Cars were abandoned in deep mud, and canoes and rowboats now ferried stranded people across flooded streets. Houses, swept off foundations, floated down the river to the ocean. They were joined by the bloated carcasses of dead animals. Telephone wires went down. The main railway to Los Angeles and the north, the Santa Fe, reported washed-out tracks. Many people were desperate to leave San Diego. "The steamship Roanoke, which sailed [Tuesday] for San Pedro and San Francisco carried 145 passengers, and the officials were forced to turn away 100 persons who tried" to escape the flooded city.

HATFIELD WAS UNAWARE OF THE HAVOC THAT WAS VISITING THE CITY.

San Diego was cut off from the rest of the United States, the rest of the world.

On Tuesday night, the first human fatalities also were reported when a boat attempting to carry two women to safety hit a submerged post and capsized. "It was pitch dark," reported the *San Diego Union*, "and although the rescuers were aided by the lanterns of those on shore, the women could not be found."

Others lost their life savings. In the early twentieth century, many folks distrusted banks so much they stuffed their money into cans, which they buried in holes around their property. The rain washed away complete hillsides, as well as people's fortunes. One tavern owner claimed to have lost $50,000 in gold when the San Diego River carried it out to sea.

At Morena, Hatfield was unaware of the havoc that was visiting the city. On Monday, he had telephoned a clerk at the water authority and told him that the rain so far was just a warm-up act to what he had planned. Then the phone went dead. He was left without a communication line or the knowledge of what was taking place sixty miles to the west.

The storm impacted not only cities along the entire Pacific coast of the United States but also those in Mexico. The mayor of Ensenada, a small fishing village in Baja California, about 83 miles south of San Diego, commented to a *Union* reporter, "It has only sprinkled in San Diego. . . . It is but a mere mist. We have had the heaviest rains in Ensenada in the memory of the oldest settler. For seven days and seven nights it not only rained, but it poured. . . . It must have been fully fifty inches!"

The public's mood changed quickly in the face of the widespread devastation. Charles Cristadoro, in a January 19 letter to the editor, asked, "Can 'Rainmaker' Hatfield be held for damages?" Cristadoro's was one voice among many.

Thursday, January 20, dawned with a shining sun and blue sky. Despite the surrounding destruction, moods were uplifted. Many suggested that it was time for Hatfield to go. However, to everyone's disappointment, the clear weather was fleeting. By Tuesday, January 25, dark, heavy clouds hung again over the Pacific Ocean and once more began making their way to land.

For the first time in its history, Morena Reservoir held more than

Closer to the city, drivers line up their vehicles on the Lower Otay Dam to celebrate the first spill over its top. Rudolph Wueste, a supervisor with the county's reservoir system, is the passenger in the middle automobile. The dam had recently been declared safe by engineers.

The Santa Fe Railway, San Diego's only rail connection to the north, reported damage to its tracks, which paralleled the coast.

ten billion gallons of water. At the dam, Swenson measured the water's depth at 137 feet. Hatfield, the cloud-attractor, unpacked a new batch of evaporating pans and continued his work dispatching a new load of chemical fumes into the air. Joel took advantage of the break in the weather to bury the used pans, raking the earth to disguise where they were hidden.

The forecast for Wednesday had been for unsettled weather into the next day. The key word was *unsettled*. Thursday's *Evening Tribune* told the story: "Wind records for San Diego were broken in last night's storm and the rainfall record for a twenty-four-hour period has been exceeded only a few times in the last fifty years." At Lower Otay Reservoir, water now was rising at almost one foot an hour, and at 5:00 p.m. Thursday, it topped the dam. This created fears that it might wash out at any minute, but city engineers had assured residents earlier that the dam was safe. As a precaution, though, residents downstream from the dam were warned to evacuate. One end of another, smaller dam—the Switzer—was dynamited to prevent the entire structure from giving way after a crack was discovered in it.

During this round of rainfall, San Diego turned into a miniature Venice, with water on Broadway, the principal roadway through the downtown business district, running at five feet deep. All around, water was rising, and all over the county, bridges that had survived the flood of a week earlier were in danger of collapse or already washed out. Indeed, a newer concrete bridge across the San Diego River that connected the southern part of the city with its far-flung northern hamlets buckled and collapsed as a new flotilla of houses and animal

Hatfield intended to give San Diego "the works" at Morena Reservoir and carried an extra chest of chemicals to get the job done.

During the second wave of flooding, a newly constructed concrete bridge gave way, cutting off San Diego from its northern neighbors. With the rail lines gone, the only way to reach the city was by ship.

Houses, swept from their foundations, floated out to the Pacific Ocean.

carcasses washed out to sea. A few hours later, the main Santa Fe railroad bridge gave way. The *Union* reported, "The . . . river, at its crest last night, was nearly six feet higher than it was early last week."

On Thursday at exactly 5:05 p.m., the Lower Otay Dam broke apart. F. E. Baird, a laborer who had volunteered to warn people in the valley below to move to higher ground, was caught by a wall of water more than forty feet high. By clinging to small trees and swimming when he could, he managed to climb to safety. He described his experience: "It was a terrible sight. . . . Trees were swept away like twigs. Nothing could have stood in the path of that seething, twisting, roaring wall of water. The noise was deafening." At 9:00 that night, the rest of the Lower Otay Dam went. The *San Diego Union* reported, "Authorities estimate that between forty and fifty persons lost their lives in the Otay valley [below the dam]. . . . Only one house out of twenty-four was left standing."

The Upper Otay Dam was declared safe. At the Sweetwater Dam, however, the earth and rock fill on either side of the concrete barrier was washed out. What remained of the dam held water seventy-eight feet deep.

"NOTHING COULD HAVE STOOD IN THE PATH OF THAT SEETHING, TWISTING, ROARING WALL OF WATER."

After the water receded, T. L. Barnes of Fenton, Barnes & Sumption Sand and Gravel Company, returned to the Otay Valley plant to survey the damage. "Steam shovels and rock crushers weighing several hundred tons have disappeared," he said. "The entire plant, erected at a cost of between $50,000 and $60,000, is a total loss. But we were not the only ones to suffer. Only a few houses remain in the valley, and these have been wrecked and removed from their former sites. . . . We were told by people on this side of the line [border] that the Tijuana [Mexico] hot springs hotel was seen floating down the river last night with the lights burning and people inside calling for help. It is believed that they were all drowned."

.   .   .

In the mountains east of San Diego on Thursday night, a nonstop rain pummeled Morena. Around midnight, dam keeper Seth Swenson struggled against the wind to maneuver a rowboat to the outlet tower that contained five valves designed to release water from the reservoir. He knew the dam could not withstand the great weight pressing against it unless he did something. Climbing deep within the tower, he turned the valves one by one. After some minutes, he heard the thundering rush of water, millions of gallons, being released into the gorge beyond the dam. But as rain continued to beat against the lake's surface, he also knew that millions of gallons more were surging into it.

As day dawned, the Hatfield brothers waded toward the dam. They were drawn by the crashing roar coming from that direction. What they saw stopped them in their tracks: water four feet deep was flowing over the top of the dam. Morena was filled to overflowing.

The rain was easing now, and Swenson checked his gauges one more time. Morena had taken in almost five billion gallons of water since the previous day's measurement.

Hatfield had fulfilled his agreement with the city. Or had he?

Although the concrete portion of the Sweetwater Reservoir Dam held, the earth and rock fill on either side washed away.

When the Lower Otay Dam gave way, almost everything in the valley below was swept away to sea. Immediate reports estimated that at least fifty lives were lost. This number was later lowered, but nobody is certain how many people died in the floods of January 1916.

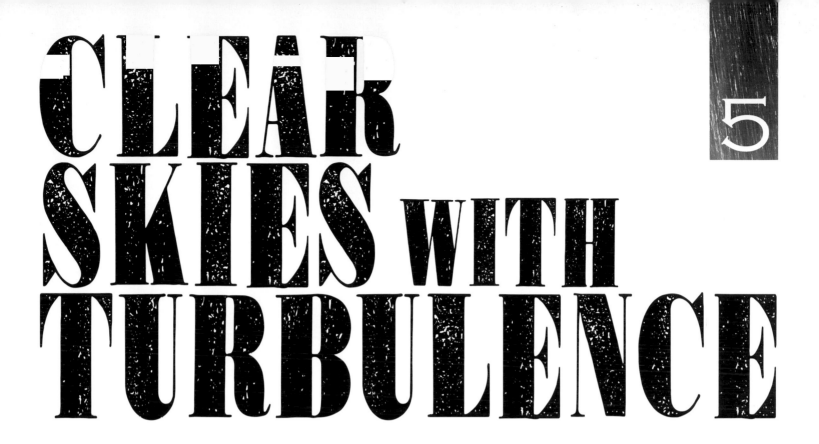

CLEAR SKIES WITH TURBULENCE

In the mountainous area around Morena, damage was minimal. With the telephone line restored, Maggie Swenson received an anonymous call on Monday, January 31. The caller threatened to lynch the Hatfield boys. Hatfield had been threatened before, but not in such serious tones. With rifles over their shoulders, Hatfield and Joel began to make their way back to the city on foot to claim their paycheck. Only then did they begin to notice the destruction. Years later, Paul described what his brothers told him they had seen on their way through the mountains: "Everything was gone. The road was gone, and bridges were gone."

Meanwhile, without word of their whereabouts, rumors began to circulate that the brothers had hightailed it to Arizona or Mexico for safety. In San Diego, people were unclear about the situation at

HERE'S HOW HATFIELD LOOKS

Charles M. Hatfield, the Man Who Claims to Have Filled Morena Dam, Engaged in Figuring on the Statement That He Will Make to the Council Monday Demanding $10,000 for His Work. Below: Joel Hatfield the Rainmaker's Brother, Who Was With Hatfield at Morena. A Front View of Charles Hatfield, and Fred A. Binney, Hatfield's Friend and Advisor. Binney Is the One With Whiskers.

Morena. Had the dam overflowed? A report in the *San Diego Union* seemed to indicate it didn't matter one way or the other. "Councilman Herbert R. Fay says the 'rainmaker' has no contract with the city and never had one. . . . The contract was never drawn . . . and Hatfield has no claim." Mrs. J. F. Rulon was a lone voice of support for Hatfield, her son-in-law. She told reporters on Monday, January 31, "If the Morena has overflown [*sic*], we may expect him here shortly. If it has not, he will remain until it does."

After four days on foot, Hatfield looked bedraggled as he checked in not with Rulon, but with Hatfield's promoter, Fred Binney. Binney found a safe place for the brothers to stay, believing them to be in danger. To scare away potential assassins, he pointed out to reporters that Hatfield was an especially quick draw with a gun. On Friday, February 4, Hatfield said to the press he would meet with city council on the following Monday, adding, "I do not anticipate that I will have any trouble in collecting what is due me. . . . I have fulfilled my part of the contract and I expect the city to fulfill its part." Once again, he attempted to shed light on his process: "When indications are favorable by the appearance of plenty of clouds my method is

84

to condense these clouds into rain instead of allowing them to pass on."

Even as City Attorney Cosgrove looked for ways to avoid paying Hatfield, others claimed the benefits of the storm offset the damages. The *Union* commented that "San Diego is assured of several—possibly five—years' supply of water, if another drop of rain does not fall this season."

The *Union* reporter who met with Hatfield on Friday described him as having the "demeanor . . . of the proverbial conquering hero, home from the fray and awaiting the laurel wreath." He added, "With Hatfield . . . was his younger brother, Joel Hatfield, who was with him at Morena during his operations." Hatfield felt assured that the city would pay him. He even offered to return to Morena to milk the clouds further in order to prove that the heavy rains of January were indeed the result of his chemical assault and not merely that of nature. Yet even more rainfall could not *really* prove he was responsible for the long, extended storm.

For its part, the U.S. Weather Bureau couldn't explain the freakish storm either. Officials there thought that it may have been due to two storms colliding over the area. Whatever the cause, the agency certainly wasn't about to give Hatfield credit for it.

Hatfield finally met with Mayor Capps and the council on Thursday, February 17. When asked what he desired from the meeting, Hatfield responded, "The essence of my contract was to fill Morena reservoir; this has been done; I have fulfilled my part of the contract and I desire that the city should fulfill its part of the contract and pay me $10,000."

Charles Hatfield and his brother Joel returned to San Diego on foot to collect their $10,000 paycheck. Pictured are Charles and, below, from left to right, Joel, Hatfield, and Fred Binney.

Before the meeting, the city attorney told the council that the city was not obligated to pay Hatfield anything. In his opinion, the rain-coaxer had delivered only some of the water that poured into Morena. Cosgrove was wrong, Hatfield complained. He explained, "I remind the council that I told them I did not claim to produce rain from a cloudless sky, but to convert a light rainfall into a heavy one, which of course implies that when I am at work nature is at work also. Therefore my contract . . . implied . . . that all natural rains coming to Morena during my operations were so much to my credit." Responding to calls that the rain-coaxer be held responsible for any damage sustained in the city, he added, "I am in no way responsible for any damage done by rains outside the Morena water shed wherein my operations were confined." Councilmen Otto Schmidt, Charles W. Fox (who replaced Henry Manney), and Herbert Fay voted against paying Hatfield. Percy Benbough and Walter Moore voted to honor the deal, but now the majority of the council refused to stand by its agreement of December.

The council's action troubled Councilman Moore. He put forward a resolution to hire Hatfield, once the Lower Otay Dam was replaced and strengthened, to keep the reservoirs "full to overflowing for the sum of $12,000 per year for five years, thereby paying him for the work he has already done and the waters he has already delivered to the city, and incidentally furnishing the city with [the] cheapest and best water of any city on the coast." In explaining his decision to propose offering a multiyear contract to Hatfield, Moore said, "I am not one bit superstitious; neither do I wish to be thought sacreligious [sic] in saying that in my opinion Mr. Hatfield can assist the Almighty

86

in his [*sic*] endeavors to beautify this, His beauty spot of America, by furnishing us an abundance of water and giving us, the citizens of San Diego, the strength of doing the rest." Moore's proposal also was turned down by the council.

City Attorney Cosgrove had earned quite a reputation for being crafty and shrewd. In addressing Moore's concern that the city was cheating Hatfield by denying him payment, Cosgrove referred to Hatfield's original offers, and then said, "The resolution which was passed by the Council simply said that Hatfield's *offer* was accepted, but it did not say which of the three propositions was accepted." In his view, and despite newspaper coverage detailing the terms, this meant the agreement had no legal merit. He also knew that if the council had admitted that Hatfield was working on behalf of San Diego, it would open the floodgates to property-damage claims, which he believed were looming. He wanted the January storms defined as acts of God, rather than acts of a municipal employee, to excuse the city from any financial responsibility.

Hatfield knew he had been beaten. Even so, he took his case to the court of public opinion by means of the newspapers. "If Council decides," he said, "through City Attorney Cosgrove's decision, to deny payment to me of my fee, it will imply that I have failed to fill Morena, which as every man, woman and child in San Diego city and county knows is untrue. The injury which this would mean to my reputation would justify me in bringing suit for heavy damages in the courts. . . . If I were a rich man, I would donate the rain to the city. I don't care about the money end of this business. Some day [*sic*] the United States

The Morena Reservoir, two years after the flood. In 1916, with all of the dam's relief valves opened, water surged over the top at a depth of four feet.

government will buy my secret and when that day arrives, I will have achieved the end I am working for—the honor of being the man who discovered how to make it rain."

In an effort to save his good name, Hatfield proposed a compromise on the morning of Monday, February 21. Meeting with the council, he said, "I am not here to demand something that does not belong to me." He agreed to settle his claim for $4,000, indicating, "My expenses for chemicals, other material and work was $3000, leaving little profit. It is not this alone that I seek. I think more of my reputation than I do of the $10,000."

"I WILL HAVE ACHIEVED THE END I AM WORKING FOR— THE HONOR OF BEING THE MAN WHO DISCOVERED HOW TO MAKE IT RAIN."

By Friday, Cosgrove had offered his view: "This office is of the opinion that the claim of Mr. Hatfield is unenforceable." He added that even if the council approved the compromise, it would not be paid by the auditor, who "will not honor an . . . [agreement] . . . which the city attorney rules is invalid."

On Monday, February 28, the *Evening Tribune* reported, "The council got rid of the Charles M. Hatfield matter this morning so far as city records are concerned by rejecting his offer to compromise."

Hatfield returned to Los Angeles, but the issue was far from forgotten. In December, a San Diego attorney representing Hatfield sat down in the city attorney's office for a meeting with Cosgrove. He had just filed suit, seeking the full $10,000. He had also just issued a summons for Mayor Capps to testify. In response to his order to appear in Superior Court, Capps commented, "Some more of the council's work; they are the fellows who bulled the whole matter."

For his part, Cosgrove had a desk piled high with claims against the city for damages that occurred during the January storms. These amounted to more than $3 million. He wasn't in a mood to authorize the city to pay Hatfield's fee or even the suggested compromise. He told Hatfield's attorney that if Hatfield would be willing to sign a statement assuming responsibility for all flood claims, he would recommend to the council that they pay Hatfield his full fee.

Hatfield could ill afford such an arrangement.

His case dragged into 1917. What he needed was for a judge or jury to decide that the storms were caused by something other than nature. However, in two cases that went to trial, the judge in each found in favor of the city council by ruling the storms were acts of God. This meant that Hatfield was relieved of any responsibility for the 1916 flood, but it also meant he would never collect a cent from San Diego.

Despite San Diego's refusal to pay the rain-coaxer, Hatfield benefited from the events of January 1916—the publicity was priceless. He found his career reignited and was soon traveling with Paul throughout the West to tickle rain into falling on parched land. An August 1919 article, "The Man the Rain Minds" in *Everybody's Magazine*, stimulated interest from Canada. When the folks in Lethbridge, Alberta, asked the U.S. Weather Bureau for its opinion of Hatfield, the agency issued a response that was so hostile that the Canadians dropped the idea of artificial rain. However, a little under one hundred miles away, in Medicine Hat, people hired him to end a five-year drought. Within days of beginning his operations, heavy rain was falling

throughout the region. When a moviemaker brought his camera and tried to film the rain-coaxer in action, Hatfield grew annoyed. To his employer, he said, "I thought I told you never to bring any movie men out here." But his employer wanted the film made. Hatfield finally agreed to go through the motions of mixing his chemicals, "but entirely different ingredients were used."

In July and August 1922, Hatfield decided "to do something I've never done before," as Paul remembered. He began experimenting with a new formula and a different approach. In Sand Canyon, on the edge of California's Mojave Desert, he set up a six-foot tower at an elevation of four thousand feet on Wednesday, July 26. He began operations at 7:30 in the morning under clear, blue skies. On Thursday, a few clouds began to form. By Saturday, a heavier bank of clouds appeared from the east and by 8:00 that evening, they completely covered the sky. By Sunday night, light sprinkles were falling and by Tuesday night, "an immense rainfall occurred at the head of Sand Canyon of cloudburst proportions." Paul recalled the Sand Canyon experiment as "one of the greatest rainfalls ever known."

Even after the San Diego fiasco, Fred Binney continued to operate on Hatfield's behalf. He began to lobby Washington to give Hatfield a job at an annual stipend of $24,000. He wanted the Division of Forestry to build a network of "Hatfield towers" to bring rain to the parched lands of the West and put an end to its dry spells. Nothing came of his efforts. Binney died in a San Diego hospital on December 5, 1927.

Always secretive, Charles Hatfield allowed cameramen to photograph him with his equipment, a stack of evaporation pans piled high on the right. But he never revealed his rain-coaxing formula, which he hoped to sell to the U.S. government.

Less than two years later, in the summer of 1929, Hatfield received an urgent telegram from the Standard Fruit and Steamship Company. Its directors wished for the rain-coaxer to travel to Central America to put out fires at their banana plantation in Honduras. The company was headquartered in New Orleans, Louisiana, and Hatfield wired right back that he was available. Paul picked up the story there. "They said if he would catch the first train, they'd hold their boat for him; so we did. We took the Sunset Limited to New Orleans . . . and went right aboard the boat and on down to Honduras. . . . We signed a contract with them for ten days and fifteen hundred dollars to put out the fire. We had the fires out in three days." Following this success, the brothers were invited to return to Honduras the next year, where they again coaxed the clouds to spill rain on lightning-caused fires.

After returning from Honduras to Los Angeles, Hatfield's wife, Maybelle, served him with divorce papers. Apparently, the relationship had been over for some time. In all the years of the couple's marriage, newspapers devoted their coverage to Hatfield with barely a mention of his wife. It was as if she was as secret as his chemical formula. Claiming verbal abuse and that he had earned $10,000 from his second trip to Honduras, which Hatfield denied, the court favored Maybelle in the divorce settlement. As reported in the *San Diego Union* on March 25, 1931, the court ordered "a division of the property and the payment of $7 per week by Hatfield for the support of" Maybelle's thirteen-year-old son. It rained the day the judge issued his decision and he quipped that he hoped it wasn't a sign of the rain-coaxer's displeasure.

In 1929, Hatfield and Paul traveled to a banana plantation in Honduras to put out lightning-caused wildfires. Here, a tower rises among the tropical fruit trees.

After their divorce, Maybelle returned to the shadows, where she had lived much of her married life, and died in 1935 at the age of fifty-four. Her children had no relationship with Hatfield.

As the 1930s continued, Hatfield would see less demand for his rain-coaxing talents. Even as the Dust Bowl raged in the central and southern plains of the United States and the country's Great Depression dragged on, leaving millions of people homeless or without jobs, the age of rainmaking was coming to an end. East of Las Vegas, Nevada, on the Colorado River, construction began on the Boulder Dam (later called Hoover Dam) in 1931 and was completed in 1936, finally guaranteeing the Southwest a reliable and an abundant source of water. On the American plains, farmers were irrigating rather than relying on nature to provide rain. Rainmaking had become a relic of the past. Hatfield returned to selling sewing machines in the Los Angeles area and married Martha McLain, a friend from his school days, in 1937.

Even though he no longer worked with a secret chemical formula, Hatfield managed to leave his mark on the history and lore of the American West. He was one of the most successful rainmakers of all time, his fame far surpassing that of Espy, Dyrenforth, Melbourne, and Jewell. On October 28, 1954, the Cort Theatre in New York premiered *The Rainmaker*, a play by N. Richard Nash. Set somewhere in the West during a time of drought, it centered on Lizzie, a plain,

HATFIELD MANAGED TO LEAVE HIS MARK ON THE HISTORY AND LORE OF THE AMERICAN WEST. HE WAS ONE OF THE MOST SUCCESSFUL RAINMAKERS IN HISTORY.

Charles Hatfield and his second wife, Martha, look over a collection of *San Diego Union* newspaper clippings about the 1916 flood.

middle-aged woman, and a mysterious rainmaker named Starbuck. The play was a hit and, in 1956, Hollywood made it into a movie starring Katharine Hepburn and Burt Lancaster. Nash admitted in an interview that as a child he'd been fascinated with rainmakers, especially Hatfield. Publicists were looking for something special for the movie's Hollywood premiere, and they found it: the rain wizard himself, then eighty-one, made an appearance.

The play has been revived often. In 1999 and 2000, Woody Harrelson appeared as Starbuck on Broadway. A musical adaptation of the play, *110 in the Shade*, with lyrics by Tom Jones and music by Harvey Schmidt, also has been popular with audiences since first appearing on Broadway in 1963.

Charles Mallory Hatfield died in the town of Pearblossom, California, on January 12, 1958, at the age of eighty-two. He took the recipe for his secret chemical brew with him to his grave. Mysterious to the end, he requested that his death not be made public. Paul honored his brother's wishes and managed to keep the story from the press for three months. Then somehow it got out, and obituaries ran in newspapers from coast to coast and across the seas.

Whether Hatfield teased the clouds into surrendering their precious liquid is another mystery. Many think he was but a gifted student of meteorology and the weather. One thing is certain: Charles Mallory Hatfield, the rain wizard, offered the drought-stricken West a glimmer of hope when hope was scarce and the times, desperate.

In a publicity photo, Charles Hatfield looks toward the sky as if conjuring up some rain.

AUTHOR'S NOTE

It seems as if I have always known the story of Charles Mallory Hatfield and his great flood in San Diego, California—the 1916 Hatfield flood. For years, though, I've wanted to dig into the facts and write about this amazing, mysterious man. Others have written about him, and I am indebted to them for telling part of the story. The more I researched, however, the more I realized that contradictions existed. For example, most recent versions of the Hatfield story indicate that Hatfield's brother Paul accompanied him to San Diego's Morena Reservoir. While digging into articles written in 1916, I learned that it was his youngest brother, Joel, who was with Hatfield at Morena, not Paul. One article even included an image of Joel, Hatfield, and Fred Binney. Although he usually acted as his brother's assistant, Paul remained in Los Angeles selling sewing machines during the Morena operation in order to earn the money that enabled Hatfield to conduct the San Diego experiments. Why does this confusion exist?

It seems that while Hatfield was alive, Paul was happy to play second fiddle, as it were, to his brother. The rain-coaxer had always received the lion's share of newspaper coverage. Around 1965, however, the story began to shift. Paul now put himself at Morena. Certainly, he would have been familiar with Hatfield's routine, having played the role of assistant for so many years. And because of their closeness, he likely would have heard his brother talk about the adventure in San Diego's backcountry. By 1965, however, Paul's sister and brothers had all died—Hatfield in 1958 and Joel, after fighting in World War I and returning to California to farm, on March 25, 1964. Their deaths were preceded by those of Stephen Girard in 1949 and Phoebe in 1953. There was no one to dispute a new version of the story.

We may never know the reason Paul put himself at Morena. Reporters simply may have assumed too much, given Paul's usual role as assistant, or it may have been easier for him to tell it as if he had been there. Whatever the reason, the details from multiple newspaper reports confirm that Joel was the brother who accompanied Hatfield into the hills of San Diego's backcountry that January of 1916. Paul died at Pearblossom in August 1974.

Also, most accounts indicate that Hatfield's father moved the family from Minnesota to San Diego shortly after the birth of Paul in 1886. They indicate that Joel was born in San Diego. However, this is at odds with Joel's birth certificate, which shows he was born in Minnesota in 1890.

Did Hatfield hold some secret formula that caused the clouds to weep? We may never know that either. What we do know is that in 1946, Vincent Schaefer, a scientist with General Electric, scattered dry ice into a bank of clouds from a plane over Schenectady, New York. Minutes later, snow fell at ground level. Nobel laureate Irving Langmuir, Schaefer's mentor, conducted experiments in cloud seeding in 1949, using generators that burned silver iodide, acetone, and propane. He found that by turning the generators on and off, he could cause rain to fall at will. Today in Africa, vase-shaped towers designed by Arturo Vittori, an industrial designer, and his colleague Andreas Vogler milk moisture from the air. Although they don't make rain in the same way that cloud seeding works, the towers, which stand thirty feet in the air, collect droplets of dew in a container at the bottom. Each provides more than twenty-five gallons per day of clean drinking water to remote villages. Perhaps Charles Hatfield was simply a man ahead of his time.

Two resources were especially helpful in crafting the book before you: *The Wizard of Sun City: The Strange True Story of Charles Hatfield, the Rainmaker Who Drowned a City's Dreams* by Garry Jenkins and *The*

In 1946, Vincent Schaefer made it snow at ground level after seeding clouds with dry ice from an airplane.

Scientist Irving Langmuir found he could make it rain at will by using generators to burn chemicals and releasing the vapors into the atmosphere.

Rainmakers: American "Pluviculture" to World War II by Clark C. Spence. The following were also invaluable: the Hatfield Papers and scrapbooks held at San Diego Public Library; Paul's two oral histories, one held at the San Diego History Center and the other at the University of California, Los Angeles; and countless newspaper articles from the *San Diego Union*, the *Evening Tribune*, the *Boston Weekly Globe*, the *San Francisco Chronicle*, the *Marion Daily Star*, the *Los Angeles Examiner*, the *Los Angeles Herald*, and the *Fort Scott Daily Monitor*. Additionally, articles from *Kiwanis* magazine, *Western Folklore*, and *Everybody's Magazine* shed light on Hatfield the rainmaker. A small booklet titled *Charles Mallory Hatfield: "The Rainmaker"* by Milford Wayne Donaldson answered many questions. The booklet was prepared for the dedication of a plaque honoring Hatfield at Morena in 1999. I am grateful to a great many people who helped me research and locate materials. They are the staff at San Diego Public Library's California Room; the staff at the San Diego History Center; Milford Wayne Donaldson, California State Historic Preservation officer (retired emeritus), Office of Historic Preservation; Sara J. Keckeisen, reference librarian, Kansas Historical Society; and (for vetting my manuscript) Kay Moore, Ed.D., professor emeritus, Teacher Education Department, California State University, Sacramento. Finally, I owe a special thanks to Paul Hatfield's grandchildren, Ty Hatfield and Karen Looker Jaramillo, who, despite busy lives, took time to clarify information and locate family memorabilia for my use.

FOR MORE INFORMATION

BOOKS

Cerveny, Randy. *Freaks of the Storm: From Flying Cows to Stealing Thunder; The World's Strangest True Weather Stories*. New York: Thunder's Mouth Press, 2006.

Crawford, Richard W. *The Way We Were in San Diego*. Charleston, SC: The History Press, 2011.

Jenkins, Garry. *The Wizard of Sun City: The Strange True Story of Charles Hatfield, the Rainmaker Who Drowned a City's Dreams*. New York: Thunder's Mouth Press, 2005.

Spence, Clark C. *The Rainmakers: American "Pluviculture" to World War II*. Lincoln: University of Nebraska Press, 1980.

FILM/VIDEO

The Rainmaker. Joseph Anthony, director; N. Richard Nash, screenwriter. Hollywood: Paramount Studios Release, 1956.

MUSIC RECORDING

110 in the Shade. Lyrics by Tom Jones; music by Harvey Schmidt. RCA Classics, October 2, 1992. Original soundtrack recording, 1963.

WEBSITES*

"Charles Hatfield." Wikipedia.
wikipedia.org/wiki/Charles_Hatfield

"Hatfield the Rainmaker" by Thomas W. Patterson. *The Journal of San Diego History*, *San Diego Historical Society Quarterly*, Winter 1970, Volume 16, Number 4. San Diego History Center.
sandiegohistory.org/journal/70winter/hatfield.htm

*Websites active at time of publication

"The Rainmaker—And Who Caused the Big Flood?" In *Gold in the Sun, 1900–1919* by Richard F. Pourade. San Diego History Center. sandiegohistory.org/books/pourade/gold/gold.htm

SOURCE NOTES

CHAPTER 1, page 6

"the first rainfall . . .": "Showers in City, County; Rain First of Season; Record Drouth Broken," *San Diego Union*, November 6, 1915.

"My brother . . .": Paul Hatfield, "Will Furnish Rain for $1000 an Inch," *San Diego Union*, March 3, 1912.

"dreadfully dry": "Hatfield Has Hemet Hypnotized," *Evening Tribune*, June 10, 1912, from *San Bernardino Sun*.

"Either he is . . .": Ibid.

"It is simply . . .": Charles Hatfield, "Seeks Contract to Produce Rain Here," *San Diego Union*, April 30, 1913.

"nature and . . .": Charles Hatfield, Ibid.

"that no harm . . .": "Water to Order from Skies Offered City by Rainmaker; $500 Asked for 5-inch Fall," *San Diego Union*, June 13, 1914.

"If Hatfield can . . .": H. A. Whitney, Ibid.

"What does he . . .": Fred Binney, "Council Prefers Providence As Rainmaker," *San Diego Union*, June 30, 1914.

"the inventor . . .": "Man Offers to Milk Skies at $1000 an Inch for Morena Reservoir," *San Diego Union*, December 8, 1915.

"$1,000 for each . . .": Ibid.

"He will have . . .": Walter Moore, "Rainmaker Finds Favor in Council; Fill Morena Reservoir for $10,000[;] Sure! Let Him Try, Moore Declares," *San Diego Union*, December 10, 1915.

"If Hatfield fills . . .": Terence Cosgrove, Ibid.

Another observer said . . . : attributed to *The Wizard of Sun City: The Strange True Story of Charles Hatfield, the Rainmaker Who Drowned a City's Dreams*, by Garry Jenkins, p. 85.

CHAPTER 2, page 28
"It was a bad time . . .": Sara J. Keckeisen, reference librarian, Kansas Historical Society, e-mail to author, June 3, 2014.

"99° in the . . .": *Fort Scott Daily Monitor*, July 16, 1875, p. 4.

"The regular train . . .": Ibid.

"Rain! rain!! rain!!! . . .": *Fort Scott Daily Monitor*, July 14, 1875, p. 4.

"The drought is . . .": "Report of the U.S. Weather Service for Week Ending December 28, 1903," *Pacific Rural Press*, January 2, 1904.

"Rainmaker Hatfield . . .": "Hatfield Hopes to Bring Water at So Much per Inch," *Los Angeles Herald*, February 3, 1904.

"When I started . . .": Charles Hatfield, "Tells How He Made Rain Come," *Los Angeles Herald*, February 7, 1904.

"I don't claim …": Charles Hatfield, Ibid.

"My process …": Charles Hatfield, Ibid.

"Weather Guesser": "Observer Franklin Thinks Storm Is Past," *Los Angeles Herald*, February 6, 1904.

"I would not say …": George E. Franklin, Ibid.

"Long live …": Ibid.

"We're satisfied …": James M. Barnett, Ibid.

"This thing …": George E. Franklin, "Hatfield and Franklin Rivals for Honor of Bringing Rain," *Los Angeles Herald*, December 3, 1904.

"Well, you do not …": Charles Hatfield, Ibid.

"His name is Hatfield …": "Mister Hatfield," by E. A. Brininstool, as it appeared in "'Natural Shower,' Forecaster Says; 'My Rain,' Says Hatfield," *Los Angeles Examiner*, December 23, 1904 (from the Hatfield Papers, San Diego Public Library).

"Wizard of Esperanza": "Hatfield Wins Prize for Rainmaking," *Los Angeles Herald*, March 30, 1905.

"Genuine 'Hatfield' Umbrellas": *The Wizard of Sun City: The Strange True Story of Charles Hatfield, the Rainmaker Who Drowned a City's Dreams*, by Garry Jenkins, p. 49.

CHAPTER 3, page 46

"40 10-foot balloons …": "Rain Made to Order," *Boston Weekly Globe*, September 8, 1891.

"Rain Made to Order" and "Gen. Dyrenforth . . ." and "Jack Rabbits . . .": Ibid.

"Whenever he ordered . . .": Ibid.

"this did not happen . . .": Ibid.

"Not Makers of Rain": "Not Makers of Rain," *San Francisco Chronicle*, October 29, 1891.

"This portion . . .": Robert St. George Dyrenforth, Ibid.

"It is the infusion . . .": Frank Melbourne, "Rain to Order," *Marion Daily Star*, July 3, 1891.

"the Rain King": Ibid.

CHAPTER 4, page 54
"to give them . . .": Paul Hatfield, "An Interview with Paul Hatfield," San Diego Historical Society Oral History Program, interviewed by Kerry Temple, December 28, 1965, p. 1.

"a compound of . . .": Rudolph Wueste, "Hatfield Contract with City Is Real," *Evening Tribune*, January 15, 1916.

"Whether Hatfield's mysterious . . .": "Rain at Morena; Did Hatfield Milk Skies?," *San Diego Union*, January 5, 1916, p. 3.

"the wrong switch" and "Official figures . . .": "Rainmaker Has No Record Yet," *Evening Tribune*, January 5, 1916, p. 6.

"Here's hoping . . .": Percy Benbough, "Is 'Rainmaker' at Work? Rain Exceeds Normal," *San Diego Union*, January 15, 1916, p. 1.

"More power to him . . .": Walter Moore, Ibid.

"Amen . . .": Herbert Fay, Ibid.

"I'll tell you . . .": Herbert Nimmo, Ibid.

"Weatherman Nimmo . . .": "Rain? Only Showers—Hatfield Fixing Up Real Downpour, Rainmaker Says," *San Diego Union*, January 18, 1916.

"him with correct data . . .": Terence Cosgrove, "'Rainmaker' Must Prove He Milked Skies—Cosgrove," *San Diego Union*, January 16, 1916, p. 29.

"He will not . . .": Terence Cosgrove, Ibid.

"seventeen and . . .": Charles Hatfield, "Hatfield Confident as Ever, Telephones from Aerie at Dam," *San Diego Union*, January 19, 1916.

"If Hatfield made . . .": "Chance for Hatfield to Grab Some Money," *Evening Tribune*, January 18, 1916.

"The steamship Roanoke . . .": "Force of Great Storm Broken; Wires Leading from City Still Down," *San Diego Union*, January 19, 1916.

"It was pitch . . .": "Two San Ysidro Women Drowned in Flood," *San Diego Union*, January 19, 1916, p. 1.

"It has only sprinkled . . .": A. Ptacnik, "Ensenada Rain Pours 7 Days," *San Diego Union*, January 27, 1916, p. 1.

"Can 'Rainmaker' Hatfield . . .": letter to the editor, Charles Cristadoro, "Can 'Rainmaker' Be Held for Damages?," *San Diego Union*, January 19, 1916.

"Wind records . . .": "Wind Records Broken; Rainfall Is Exceeded Few Times in 50 Years," *Evening Tribune*, January 27, 1916, p. 5.

"The . . . river . . .": "Dams Holding Against Great Floods as Wires Go; City Supply All Right," *San Diego Union*, January 28, 1916, p. 1.

"It was a terrible sight . . .": F. E. Baird, "Valley Is Warned[;] Risks Life to Save Others," *San Diego Union*, January 28, 1916, p. 9.

"Authorities estimate . . .": "Lower Otay Dam Gone; May Be 50 Dead; Relief Started; Water Supply Assured," *San Diego Union*, January 29, 1916, p. 1.

"Steam shovels . . .": T. L. Barnes, "Flood Destroys Big Gravel Plant," *San Diego Union*, January 29, 1916, p. 14.

CHAPTER 5, page 82

"Everything was gone. . . .": Paul Hatfield, "The Hatfield Brothers, Rainmakers," Oral History Program, University of California, Los Angeles, interviewed by James V. Mink, May 7–9, 1969, p. 65.

"Councilman Herbert R. Fay . . .": "Hatfield to Stay on Job Until Dam Overflows, Plan," *San Diego Union*, February 1, 1916, p. 8.

"If the Morena . . .": Mrs. J. F. Rulon, Ibid.

"I do not anticipate . . .": Charles Hatfield, "City to Pay for Water Hatfield Claims," *Evening Tribune*, February 4, 1916.

"When indications . . .": Charles Hatfield, Ibid.

"San Diego is assured . . .": "Great Benefit from Rain Shown by Reports from All over Back Country," *San Diego Union*, February 5, 1916.

"demeanor . . . of the proverbial . . .": "Hatfield Bobs Up with Claim for Recent Rains," *San Diego Union*, February 5, 1916.

"The essence . . .": Charles Hatfield, "Hatfield Claim Is Rejected by Council,"
   Evening Tribune, February 18, 1916.

"I remind the council . . .": Charles Hatfield, Ibid.

"I am in no way . . .": Charles Hatfield, Ibid.

"full to over flowing . . .": Walter Moore, "Wants Hatfield Hired by Year," *Evening
   Tribune*, February 18, 1916.

"I am not . . .": Walter Moore, Ibid.

"The resolution . . .": Terence Cosgrove, "Hatfield Is Refused Payment by Council,"
   San Diego Union, February 18, 1916.

"If Council decides . . .": Charles Hatfield, "Hatfield Asserts He Will Sue City for
   Rain Claim," *San Diego Union*, February 20, 1916.

"I am not here . . .": Charles Hatfield, "Rainmaker Is Willing to Take $4000,"
   Evening Tribune, February 21, 1916.

"My expenses for . . .": Charles Hatfield, Ibid.

"This office is . . .": Terence Cosgrove, "'Rainmaker's' Claim Up to City Council,"
   San Diego Union, February 26, 1916.

"will not honor . . .": Terence Cosgrove, Ibid.

"The council got rid . . .": "Council Turns Rainmaker Down," *Evening Tribune*,
   February 28, 1916.

"Some more of . . .": Edward Capps, "Hatfield Sues for $10,000," *Evening Tribune*,
   December 2, 1916, p. 10.

"I thought I told . . .": Charles Hatfield, "Movie Operator Tries to 'Shoot' the Rain-Maker," undated, unattributed newspaper article from the Hatfield Scrapbooks, San Diego Public Library.

"but entirely . . .": "Movie Operator Tries to 'Shoot' the Rain-Maker," undated, unattributed newspaper article from the Hatfield Scrapbooks, San Diego Public Library.

"to do something . . .": Charles Hatfield, as remembered by Paul Hatfield, "The Hatfield Brothers, Rainmakers," Oral History Program, University of California, Los Angeles, interviewed by James V. Mink, May 7–9, 1969, p. 116.

"an immense rainfall . . .": Paul Hatfield, Ibid., p. 142.

"one of the . . .": Paul Hatfield, Ibid., p. 116.

"They said if . . .": Paul Hatfield, Ibid., p. 112.

"a division of . . .": "Rainmaker Single Again; Sued by Wife," *San Diego Union*, March 25, 1931, p. 13.

INDEX

Page numbers in **boldface** refer to photographs and/or captions.

PICTURE CREDITS

For information about permission to reproduce selections from this book, please contact permissions@highlights.com.

Calkins Creek

An Imprint of Highlights

815 Church Street

Honesdale, Pennsylvania 18431

Printed in China

ISBN: 978-1-59078-990-2

Library of Congress Control Number: 2015931581

First edition

10 9 8 7 6 5 4 3 2 1

Designed by Barbara Grzeslo

Production by Sue Cole

Titles set in Brie Regular

Text set in Gill Sans Light